IMPRESSIONISM

★ IN MY GALLERY ★

WRITTEN BY
EMILIE DUFRESNE

DESIGNED BY
DANIELLE RIPPENGILL

BookLife
PUBLISHING

©2020
BookLife Publishing Ltd.
King's Lynn
Norfolk PE30 4LS

A catalogue record for this book is available from the British Library.

ISBN: 978-1-78637-847-7

Written by:
Emilie Dufresne

Edited by:
Madeline Tyler

Designed by:
Danielle Rippengill

IMAGE CREDITS

COVER AND THROUGHOUT – ARTBESOURO, APRIL_PIE, SHTONADO, TASHANATASHA, HAPPYPICTURES, JUDYJUMP, YULIYA DARAFEI. BACKGROUNDS – EXPRESSVECTORS. GABE & ARTISTS – GRINBOX. GALLERY – GOODSTUDIO, SIBERIAN ART. 2 – FOCUS_BELL, GRINBOX, STOCKVECTOR. 5 – SWEET ART. 8 – ONYXPRJ, NOTIONPIC. 9 – KARAKOTSYA, EVERETT - ART. 10&11 – EVERETT - ART. 14&15 – STOCKVECTOR. 17 – NIKITEEV_KONSTANTIN. 18&19 – YULIYA DARAFEI, OLGA_C, SHAKABRA. 22&23 – HASIRU. 28&29 – YULIYA DARAFEI, GRINBOX, OLGABERLET, HASIRU. IMAGES ARE COURTESY OF SHUTTERSTOCK.COM. WITH THANKS TO GETTY IMAGES, THINKSTOCK PHOTO AND ISTOCKPHOTO.

CONTENTS

Words that look like **this** are explained in the glossary on page 31.

WELCOME TO THE GALLERY

Hello, I'm Gabe. I work in this gallery and it is my job to learn about and create artworks in the style of Impressionism.

Museums and Galleries

Museums and galleries are buildings that contain art or **artefacts**. They look after the artworks and show them to the public. They can put on exhibitions and shows to display their art to the public.

TYPES OF ART

There are lots of different types of art, such as **sculpture**, **installation art** and **performance art**. The Impressionists were mostly known for their paintings. This means we need to know how to describe the **techniques** that painters use when creating their art.

Brushstrokes are the marks that are made by a tool, such as a paintbrush, being dragged across the **canvas**. There are many different types of brushstroke, such as short and thick or long and smooth.

Impasto is when paint is layered thickly onto a canvas so that it sticks out from the surface rather than being smooth and flat.

Optical mixing is when an artist puts two colours next to each other on a canvas to give the idea that the colours are mixing rather than mixing them together on a **palette**.

IMPRESSIONISM WING

Welcome to the Impressionism Wing! It may be empty at the moment, but soon this wing will be filled with amazing paintings in the styles of different Impressionist artists.

Some museums or galleries only show one type of art, or art from one particular artist. This gallery has different areas of the building for different art <u>movements</u>. This wing will show Impressionist work.

This wing is going to be full of paintings, so we need to make sure there is lots of wall space to hang them. I think that curved wall at the back would be perfect for a very impressive painting I have in mind.

BEFORE THE MID-1800s, GALLERIES WOULD OFTEN SHOW ALL THE ART THEY OWNED AT ONCE. THIS MEANT THAT PICTURES WERE OFTEN HUNG ON TOP OF EACH OTHER AND TOOK UP MOST OF THE WALL SPACE. AFTER THE MID-1800s, PAINTINGS WERE MORE SPREAD OUT AND HAD MORE SPACE AROUND THEM.

Before we start creating art in the style of Impressionism, let's learn some more about the movement.

WHAT IS IMPRESSIONISM?

Before Impressionism

Before Impressionism, there was an art movement called Realism. Realist paintings often showed everyday people in everyday positions. Before this, paintings were often of very grand or impressive things and rich people would often <u>pose</u> for the painting.

RICH PERSON POSING

EVERYDAY PERSON DOING EVERYDAY THINGS

Realism was the first movement where <u>working-class</u> people were shown doing everyday things, such as working or cleaning. Realist paintings were often of the city or the countryside, and would show the working classes going about their lives.

What Common People Do

Realism influenced Impressionism – Impressionist artists also wanted to show <u>landscapes</u> and scenes of everyday things. Impressionism began in Paris in the 1860s. At this time, lots of railway lines were being built to the French countryside from Paris. This meant that artists could travel there to paint.

IMPRESSIONIST LANDSCAPE PAINTING

IMPRESSIONIST <u>PORTRAIT</u> PAINTING

During this time, Paris was changing; more and more <u>middle-class</u> people could sit outside and enjoy getting together in the streets. Many Impressionist painters chose to show these scenes in their work. Whether this was eating lunch in a park, having a drink or walking to work, the everyday was still being shown in Impressionist works.

One Moment in Time

There were some differences between Realism and Impressionism, and one of these was how artists painted these scenes. The Impressionists were not worried about making a scene look real. Instead, they wanted to show what they saw in the blink of an eye or give the impression, or idea, of a moment in time. This is why they became known as the Impressionists.

Impressionist artists also tried to show light in paintings in a different way to how it had been done before. Much like how they wanted to show one moment in time, the Impressionists also wanted to show how they saw light in one moment. This also made the paintings look less like Realist paintings.

Movement and Brushstrokes

Impressionist artists also tried to show movement in their paintings. Rather than being set up or posed, the artists would often paint outside in public spaces. The way they showed light in their paintings helped to give the impression of movement in the painting. Impressionists were also very revolutionary in how they put paint onto the canvas. They often used impasto and their short, thick brushstrokes could be seen. The Impressionists were known for using brighter colours than the movements that had come before them.

EDGAR DEGAS

Country of Birth: France
Born: 1834
Died: 1917 (aged 83)

Edgar Degas was born in Paris. He went to a very **prestigious** school to study art before travelling to Italy to study **Renaissance** art by artists such as Leonardo Da Vinci and Michelangelo.

Degas started as a Realist artist, but he soon began to create paintings of modern life in Paris. He painted scenes at horse races and at the opera. Unlike other Impressionists of the time, Degas would not create landscape paintings. Instead he focused more on people and how they went about their everyday lives. In particular, he liked to show people in unusual positions, such as ballet dancers stretching or women trying on hats. This allowed him to give the impression of lots of movement in his paintings.

Degas was very important in the Impressionist movement and is part of the group of artists who began the **Modern Art** period. He is believed to have influenced Pablo Picasso and Henri Matisse.

Activity:
STILL BUT MOVING

You will need:

A camera ☑

A printer ☑

Paper ☑

Wax crayons ☑

Let's try to create a piece of art that shows movement and light, just like Degas.

First, you need to take some photos. I am going to take some of me and my friends dancing, but you could take photos of any kind of movement you want, such as people playing sport.

Choose your favourite photo. Now print it off in black and white. Use the crayons to colour in the picture. Try to use short, thick lines just like the Impressionists did.

Keep looking at the photo to see where the light hits the people's bodies. Use lighter colours such as white and cream where the light falls.

Don't worry about colouring inside the lines. Impressionist paintings often looked blurry because they were trying to show movement.

Next, I'll add more light colours to really make it look like a fleeting moment, and then I'm finished.

CLAUDE MONET

Country of Birth: France
Born: 1840
Died: 1926 (aged 86)

Claude Monet is seen as the <u>pioneer</u> and leader of Impressionism. Although Monet began painting people, he is mostly known for his landscape paintings. He often painted 'en plein air' which means 'in open air' in French. He would often choose one subject, such as haystacks, cathedrals or waterlilies, and then paint them over and over again. He would paint them at different times of day and in different types of weather. This changed how the natural light made the landscape look. Throughout his career, Monet painted around 250 paintings just of waterlilies.

Many people see Monet as a very important figure in Modern Art, who changed the way artists expressed themselves in paintings forever by becoming more <u>abstract</u> and <u>expressive</u> in the way he painted.

Activity:

SPONGY LANDSCAPES

You will need:

Thick card or paper of any size you want ☑

Something hard and flat to lean on ☑

Sponges ☑

Paints in different colours ☑

Paintbrushes ☑

It's time to grab your paint and equipment. We are off to paint en plein air!

First, put all the things you need into a bag and go outside – this could be the local park, a forest or your garden.

I have used this very big piece of paper because I want this to be a large painting that stretches across the curved wall of the gallery, but you can use any size you want. Now use your sponges to paint the background. I'm painting a picture of some boats on a lake, so I am mostly mixing blues and greens on my background.

Once your background is dry, get your paintbrushes out and add in some more detail. There were some boats on the lake and some buildings to the right, so I will add those in with paint. What details could you add to your painting?

19

PIERRE-AUGUSTE RENOIR

Country of Birth: France
Born: 1841
Died: 1919 (aged 78)

Pierre-August Renoir began painting pottery in a factory before moving to Paris to study painting techniques. While studying, he met Claude Monet. It was not long until Renoir's work began to change and look more Impressionist. Like Degas, Renoir's Impressionist paintings were often of people outside and living their modern lives. In his work, he tried to show that sunlight falling on people's skin looked luminous or glowing, and sunlight falling though the leaves of plants looked as though it was sparkling.

Later in his career, Renoir stopped creating Impressionist artworks and his work changed. Instead of using short brushstrokes, he began to create paintings with stronger and clearer edges to all the objects. However, he still used light colours, which he got from the Impressionists.

21

Activity:
WATERCOLOURS AND WAX

You will need:

Wax crayons ☑

A glass of water ☑

Watercolour paints ☑

Paintbrushes ☑

Thick paper or card ☑

A camera ☑

We are going to try to create a painting in the style of Renoir using a technique called <u>wax resist</u>.

Go outside to a space with some nice plants or trees. Take a photo of your friends or people you know near the plants. When you're back inside, get ready to draw.

First, sketch out a drawing of the picture. Use the wax crayons to colour in the picture, but not the background. Make sure you add in any details you want to stand out using the crayons.

Once you are happy with your drawing, get your watercolours. Choose the colours you want to be in your background. Brush them across the whole of your painting. Don't be nervous about painting over the wax crayons – the crayons will resist the paint! Once you are happy, let your painting dry. Now you have a painting in the style of Renoir.

MARY CASSATT

Country of Birth: US
Born: 1844
Died: 1926 (aged 82)

Mary Cassatt was born in the US but travelled to Europe to study. She created art while travelling and had one of her pieces accepted at an exhibition. Edgar Degas saw the exhibition and asked her to show her work alongside the Impressionists.

Cassatt preferred to show people instead of landscapes in her artwork. However, her pieces of people were different to other Impressionist works of the time. Cassatt chose to show women from inside their homes in her artworks. She showed mothers and children sitting together, or women reading or having tea.

Cassatt helped to spread the ideas of Impressionism from Europe to the US. She would ask her friends in the US to buy Impressionist artworks from Europe. In fact, many of these works make up part of a collection in the Metropolitan Museum in New York City.

Activity:
PASTEL SELF-PORTRAITS

You will need:

Pastels in various colours ☑

A pencil ☑

Thick paper or card ☑

A camera ☑

A friend ☑

Mary Cassatt was known for using pastels to create her pieces. Let's try and create a self-portrait using Cassatt's techniques!

Sit down and do something that you do quite a lot, such as having a drink or looking at your tablet or computer. Try not to pose — just sit as you usually would. Get a friend to take a picture of you doing this.

Now recreate your photo. First, sketch it out using your pencil. Once you are happy with your sketch, it's time to get your pastels out. Cassatt was known for using light colours so I'm going to use light colours, too. The fun thing about pastels is you can use your fingers to mix colours together or layer them.

I have blurred some white bits into the other colours using my finger, just like the Impressionists did. Now I just need to finish off adding in the other colours and it will be ready for the gallery!

OPENING NIGHT

How do you think the wing looks now it is full of art? It's great to see everyone talking about the artworks! Let's see what they are saying...

There are no right or wrong answers when you are talking about a piece of art, or how it makes you feel. What do you think of these pieces? Which is your favourite, and why? Are there any that make you feel happy or sad?

QUIZ

1. What art movement came before Impressionism?
2. Around what time did galleries stop showing all their paintings at once?
3. Which artist liked to show people moving in unusual positions?
4. Who was known for painting landscapes en plein air?
5. Which artist was known for using pastels to create their works?

Answers: 1. Realism **2.** Mid-1800s **3.** Edgar Degas **4.** Claude Monet **5.** Mary Cassatt

You could try and go to a gallery or museum near you.

It might **inspire** you to create some more art. There are loads of different art movements and styles to try. You could even find your own way of creating art and start a whole new movement! Don't forget to ask the people you are with how the artworks make them feel.

We want to see your artworks! If you do any of these activities, why not put it on social media and use #InMyGalleryImpressionism so that we can see what you have created!

GLOSSARY

abstract	art that doesn't try to show something as it looks in real life
artefacts	objects made by humans in history
canvas	a woven fabric that is pulled tightly over a frame to create a blank space to be painted on
expressive	showing feelings and emotions
inspire	to influence to do something
installation art	art that people have to interact with by either walking around, touching or listening to
landscapes	scenes that include nature, such as fields, mountains or oceans
middle-class	a class of people who are in between the upper class and working class
Modern Art	a period of time from around 1850 to 1970 that includes many art movements and represents when artists began moving away from traditional art
movements	categories or types of art that an artwork or artist might belong to, which can sometimes be related to a certain time or place
palette	a piece of equipment that an artist may use to mix colours
performance art	a type of art that is often performed live to viewers or spectators
pioneer	the first person to do something new or in a new way
portrait	a painting, drawing or photograph of a person
pose	to hold yourself in a certain way for a period of time, usually for a photograph or painting
prestigious	having an important and highly regarded status
Renaissance	a period of time from the 14th to the 17th century when European art and literature became popular again
revolutionary	doing something in a way that completely changes how it was done or thought of before
sculpture	a decorative object made through carving, chiselling or moulding
sketch	to do a quick drawing, often in pencil
techniques	particular ways of doing something
wax resist	an art technique that involves using wax crayons to draw a picture before painting over it with watercolours; the wax resists the watercolour paint and the picture can be seen through the paint
working-class	a class of people who make up the main workforce in a society

INDEX